WORLD'S
SCARIEST
PREDATORS

T0102254

PREDATORS OF
South America
and Antarctica

Michael Tylers

Cavendish
Square
New York

Published in 2015 by Cavendish Square Publishing, LLC
243 5th Avenue, Suite 136, New York, NY 10016

Copyright © 2015 by Cavendish Square Publishing, LLC

First Edition

No part of this publication may be reproduced, stored in a retrieval system, or transmitted in any form or by any means—electronic, mechanical, photocopying, recording, or otherwise—without the prior permission of the copyright owner. Request for permission should be addressed to Permissions, Cavendish Square Publishing, 243 5th Avenue, Suite 136, New York, NY 10016. Tel (877) 980-4450; fax (877) 980-4454.

Website: cavendishsq.com

This publication represents the opinions and views of the author based on his or her personal experience, knowledge, and research. The information in this book serves as a general guide only. The author and publisher have used their best efforts in preparing this book and disclaim liability rising directly or indirectly from the use and application of this book.

CPSIA Compliance Information: Batch #WW15CSQ

All websites were available and accurate when this book was sent to press.

Library of Congress Cataloging-in-Publication Data

Tylers, Michael, 1959- author.
Predators of South America and Antarctica / Michael Tylers.
pages cm. — (World's scariest predators)
Includes bibliographical references and index.
ISBN 978-1-50260-182-7 (hardcover) ISBN 978-1-50260-181-0 (paperback) ISBN 978-1-50260-180-3 (ebook)
1. Predatory animals—South America—Juvenile literature. 2. Predatory animals—Antarctica—Juvenile literature. 3. Predation (Biology)—Juvenile literature. I. Title.

QL758.T96 2015
591.53—dc23

2014024983

Editor: Kristen Susienka
Senior Copy Editor: Wendy A. Reynolds
Art Director: Jeffrey Talbot
Designer: Douglas Brooks
Senior Production Manager: Jennifer Ryder-Talbot
Production Editor: David McNamara
Photo Researcher: J8 Media

The photographs in this book are used by permission and through the courtesy of:
Nick Gibson/Getty Images, 4; Dreamstime: 8 (Matthew G. Simpson), 8 (Morten Elm), 9 (Steffen Foerster),
12 (Rhallam), 16 (Ammit), 20 (Fanny Reno), 24 (Designpicssub) 28 (Cathy Kiefer), 29 (Dirk Ercken),
FLPA: 12 (Flip Nicklin), 13 (Hiroya Minakuchi), 21 (Mike Parry), 24, 25 both (Thierry Montford),
Photos.com: 16, 17, Public Domain: 28.

Printed in the United States of America

Contents

	Introduction	5
Birds:	Frigate Bird	6
Mammals:	Leopard Seal	10
	Jaguar	14
Reptiles:	Leatherback Turtle	18
	Vine Snake	22
Amphibians:	Red-Eyed Tree Frog	26
	Glossary	30
	Find Out More	31
	Index	32

Did You Know?

One in ten animals in the world live in South America's large Amazon rain forest.

Introduction

The world is full of many animals. They are not all the same, though. Some animals have lots of fur and four legs, while others have wings and can fly. Some animals eat plants, and some hunt for other animals to live. It is these hunting animals that can sometimes strike fear into the hearts of people.

South America and Antarctica have many animals, including birds, frogs, snakes, seals, and jaguars. Some of these animals are very big, and some have large claws and sharp teeth. Others are small but they have poisonous skin or the ability to blend in with their surroundings.

This book will provide some amazing facts about some of the scariest and most interesting animals in South America and Antarctica. Remember that animals are nearby no matter where you live. Keep your eyes open and you will be sure to see some of them. Just be sure not to get too close.

BIRDS
Frigate Bird

Scientific Name: Genus *Fregata*

The frigate bird is a very special bird. It spends almost its entire life flying. In fact, it can stay airborne for up to a week, stopping only to roost during the mating season! The frigate bird flies so much because it cannot swim, unlike other birds that live by the sea. Instead, it flies low above the water, waiting for the right moment to scoop up its **prey**. Using its hooked beak, it can snatch fish, crabs, squid, and even small sea turtles out of the water in seconds. This technique needs skill and daring. One error can be fatal. Although the frigate bird flies for much of its life, it tends to stay within 100 miles (160 kilometers) of land.

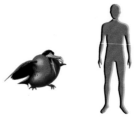

Scale

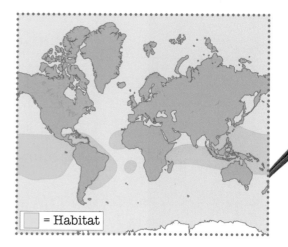

= Habitat

Where in the World?

Frigate birds live around tropical islands and waters, mostly in the Pacific Ocean, but occasionally are seen in the Indian and Atlantic oceans as well.

Wings

The frigate bird's wings are enormous. A male's wingspan can measure up to 8 feet (2.4 meters). With wings this large, the bird can fly for a long time without using up a lot of energy.

Gular pouch

Male frigate birds have a bright red throat pouch, called a gular pouch, which they inflate to attract females during the mating season.

Feet

Although the frigate bird's feet are tiny compared to the rest of its body, all four toes on the frigate bird's feet are webbed.

Tail

A long, forked tail gives the bird balance and helps it fly. The shape of the tail allows it to twist and turn through the air.

Frigate birds are thought to be closely related to another seabird called the pelican because of how they look and how they fly.

A male frigate bird puffs out his gular pouch.

Ferocious Fact

Male and female frigate birds are colored differently. Females are usually black with white on their chests and underneath, while males are all black except for their throat pouch, which is red and can puff out to the size of a person's head.

Frigate birds often hunt food as they fly.

Did You Know?

- There are five different species of frigate birds. The Magnificent frigate bird is the largest, while the Least frigate bird is the smallest.

- A favorite food of the Magnificent frigate bird is flying fish.

- Young frigate birds drop items such as feathers in midair and practice catching them to prepare for when they are old enough to hunt for themselves.

- Frigate birds are also called man-o'-war birds.

Frigate birds never stray far from land.

Leopard Seal

Scientific Name: *Hydrurga leptonyx*

The leopard seal is sometimes called the sea leopard because it is such a good hunter. In fact, it is one of Antarctica's top sea **predators**, second only to the killer whale. Most seals eat fish and **crustaceans**, but the leopard seal also enjoys eating warm-blooded prey. It regularly hunts smaller species of seals, but penguins are its favorite food. The seal will wait until penguins enter the water. Then, when it strikes, it moves with amazing speed. When it gets hold of its prey, it shakes it like a rag doll, shredding the victim into bite-sized chunks. Although leopard seals usually do not eat humans, if threatened, they will attack.

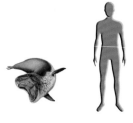

Scale

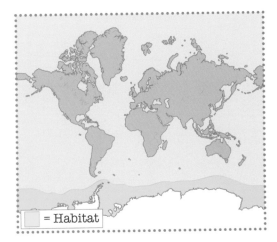

= Habitat

Where in the World?

Leopard seals are found along the coast of Antarctica and around most sub-Antarctic islands, especially where penguins breed. However, some venture as far north as South America and New Zealand in search of food.

Body
Leopard seals grow up to 12 ft (3.6 m) long. Their long bodies are designed to make them fast and graceful in the water.

Flippers
Leopard seals swim using long, powerful strokes of their front flippers. However, they are clumsy on land, and move by wriggling their flippers and stomach muscles.

Skin
Like most species of seal, leopard seals are kept warm by a thick layer of fat under the skin known as **blubber**.

Teeth
Large, sharp front teeth are designed to capture and shred prey, while back teeth, called molars, have sharp edges, but are connected in a way that lets the seal sift **krill**.

Leopard seals gather in groups to find a mate.

Ferocious Fact

Leopard seals tend to live alone and only gather in groups when it is time to mate. Mothers and their babies, called pups, spend time in water and on land. Unlike other species, the female leopard seals are larger and heavier than the males. They can reach 12 feet (3.6 m) in length and weigh almost 1,000 pounds (450 kg).

The leopard seal might look cute, but it's a deadly predator.

A leopard seal attacks hikers who get too close.

Did You Know?

- The leopard seal weighs between 800 and 1,000 lbs (362–450 kg).

- Leopard seals play the same role as polar bears in the Arctic. They are fierce predators of other animals.

- Leopard seals also get their name for the spots they have on their coat, which look like leopard spots.

- They may be clumsy on land, but in the water leopard seals can swim at speeds of up to 25 mph (40 kmh).

Leopard seals are expert swimmers.

Jaguar

Scientific Name: *Panthera onca*

The jaguar is an excellent hunter. It looks similar to a leopard, but is shorter, more muscular, and much stronger. For instance, a jaguar can drag an 800-pound (362-kilogram) bull in its jaws and crush its bones easily! Most jaguars live in rain forests, where they feed on tree-dwelling monkeys and small alligator-like animals called caimans. In areas near to humans, they use their eyesight, hearing, and sense of smell to hunt when it's dark. In more rural regions, they hunt just before dawn. Usually, they sneak up on their victims, taking them completely by surprise and suffocating them with a bite to the throat. All of these factors put the jaguar at the top of the South American food chain.

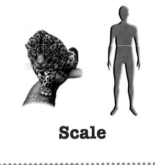

Scale

☐ = Habitat

Where in the World?

Although they were once common throughout the Americas, jaguars are now mainly found in Brazil, Paraguay, and Belize. Over the years, jaguars have vanished from 40 percent of their historical areas, mostly because of being hunted by humans for their coats.

Eyes

Jaguars have better vision in low light because a mirror-like structure at the back of the eye reflects light into an area called the **retina**.

Claws

Long, curved, retractable claws pin down and kill prey. One swipe can kill an animal the size of a dog.

Jaws

Most big cats kill with a bite to the throat. The jaguar's jaws are so strong that it can also kill its victims by piercing the prey's skull.

Fur

Dark spots on the fur, called rosettes, help the jaguar blend in with the spotted light of its forest home. In areas with lots of forest trees, its coat is darker.

Ferocious Fact

Jaguars are one of the big cats that can roar, like the tiger, lion, and leopard. This is because a part of their throat called the **larynx** is enlarged. The bigger the larynx is, the louder the cat can roar. Some people describe a jaguar's roar as a deep cough.

Jaguars are the largest of South America's big cats.

Jaguars are often hunted for their beautiful fur.

A jaguar sneaks up on a caiman swimming through the water.

Did You Know?

- Jaguars are the third-largest cats on Earth and listed as an endangered species. Humans hunt them every year and make their population decrease. If this trend continues, jaguars may become extinct.

- One of the native names for this cat is *yaguareté*, which means "true fierce beast."

- The rosettes on the jaguar's coat are like fingerprints. Each cat has a different pattern. Some rosettes may include one or more dots, and their shapes, sizes, and colors vary.

No two jaguars have the same markings on their coat.

Leatherback Turtle

Scientific Name: *Dermochelys coriacea*

The leatherback turtle is a **prehistoric** animal whose ancestors once shared the planet with dinosaurs. Today, it is the largest turtle on Earth. On land, it is slow and vulnerable, but in water it is a swift and graceful hunter. A leatherback can weigh as much as 2,000 pounds (907 kg), and a body that size needs a lot of fuel. It preys on species such as the lion's mane jellyfish. In fact, the leatherback consumes around 73 percent of its body weight every day in jellyfish. When it is time to lay eggs, female turtles return to the beaches where they were born. Only one out of one thousand leatherbacks makes it to adulthood.

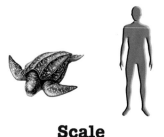

Scale

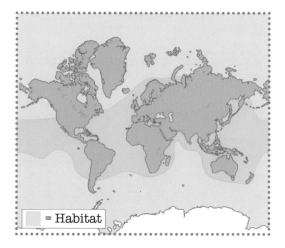

= Habitat

Where in the World?

Leatherback turtles were once one of the most widespread species of reptiles. Today they can be found in the Atlantic, Indian, and Pacific oceans, as far north as Norway and as far south as New Zealand.

Carapace (Shell)

The leatherback is unique because its upper body is covered by thick skin containing bony deposits that protect the turtle and make its shell feel leathery to the touch.

Mouth

This turtle doesn't have teeth. Instead, it has tooth-like cusps on its upper jaw. Backward-facing spines in its throat help the turtle swallow food.

Body

Seven ridges run along the turtle's back. These make the leatherback's body move through the water more easily.

Flippers

The leatherback turtle's front flippers can grow up to 8 ft 10 in (2.7 m) long. The turtle uses these to propel itself through the water.

Leatherback turtles are the largest turtles on Earth.

Baby Leatherbacks, called hatchlings, are about 4 inches (10.6 cm) long when born.

Ferocious Fact

Reptiles warm their bodies by sitting in the sun. This means that they struggle to survive in extreme temperatures, especially the cold. Leatherback turtles handle the cold much better than other reptiles thanks to layers of fat under their skin. This keeps them warm in chilly waters.

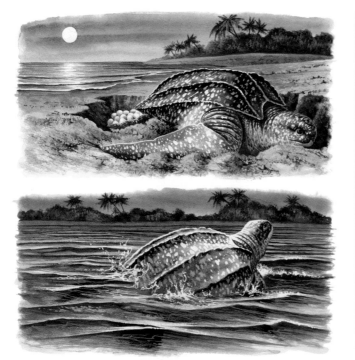

Did You Know?

- After they are born, male turtles spend their whole lives at sea. Females only set foot —or flipper—on land to lay their eggs.

- Leatherback turtles are expert divers. They can dive to depths of 4,200 ft (1,280 m) and stay down for as long as eighty-five minutes.

- Leatherbacks often mistake plastic bags for jellyfish. These can kill the turtle if eaten.

A female Leatherback climbs ashore to lay her eggs.

While a female will lay around eighty eggs, only a few hatchlings live to adulthood.

Vine Snake

Scientific Name: Genus _Oxybelis_

Hunting by day from its perch in the trees, the vine snake is a skilled predator. It can slowly **stalk** its prey and spring upon it when it least expects. With its long, slender shape and tree-colored body, it easily blends in with its surroundings. While many snake species flick their tongue rapidly in and out of their mouth, vine snakes hold their tongues outside the mouth and move it slowly. No one knows for certain why, but some scientists think the snake uses its tongue to lure its prey in the same way a fisherman puts a worm on a hook. Once it has made a catch, few animals escape that large mouth!

Scale

= Habitat

Where in the World?

Vine snakes range from the southern United States to South America as far as Peru. The Roatan snake is a native of Roatan Island. Generally, green vine snakes inhabit rain forests. Browner species live in savannahs and dry forests.

Eyes

A narrow head means the snake's eyes point almost forward. Many other species of snake have eyes placed on the sides of their heads.

Body

The long, thin body may grow up to 6 ft (1.8 m). The snake's tail makes up more than one-third of the reptile's body length.

Color

There are four known species of vine snake in the genus *Oxybelis*. Body color may vary from green, yellow-brown, or brown, with a yellowish or white underside.

Mouth & Fangs

The vine snake's mouth spans almost the whole length of its head. Two grooved teeth at the back of its mouth direct poisonous saliva into wounds.

Vine snakes rely on camouflage to survive in their environment.

Ferocious Fact

While there are only four types of known *Oxybelis* vine snakes, there are other vine snake species around the world. Each species is slightly different, but they all have similarities. All have their fangs at the back of their mouth. By opening their mouths wide, this allows them to inject venom, or poison, from their teeth into their victims.

A vine snake opens its mouth wide to reveal its sharp, deadly fangs.

Did You Know?

- There are four known species of vine snakes in the genus *Oxybelis*. These are Cope's vine snake, the green vine snake, the Mexican vine snake, and the Roatan vine snake.

- It has been reported that when it attacks large prey, the vine snake will bite into its victim's head and hold it off the ground to stop it from struggling.

- Green vine snakes are such fast and skillful predators that they can catch hummingbirds!

Vine snakes lay very still before catching food such as hummingbirds.

Vine snakes have thin bodies and wide mouths.

Red-Eyed Tree Frog

Scientific Name: *Agalychnis callidryas*

By day, this brightly colored frog stays out of sight, sleeping on the underside of leaves, with its eyes closed and its blue flashes hidden by its feet. At night, when its bright green coloration is covered in darkness, it comes out to feed. The red-eyed tree frog is a strict **carnivore** with special characteristics that help it hunt. Its long legs and suckers on each digit allow it to climb with ease. Its feet are partially **webbed**, making it a good swimmer. It has excellent eyesight to locate prey. It can even change its body color to blend in with its surroundings. In fact, despite all appearances, this little frog is a fast and skillful predator.

Scale

☐ = Habitat

Where in the World?

Red-eyed tree frogs prefer habitats that are close to water, which they need to breed. They are found in American rain forests from southern Mexico to northern Colombia. They are also popular pets.

Feet

The tree frog's feet are large and flexible. Sticky pads on its digits help it to grip onto leaves and trees. The frog's partially webbed feet help it to swim.

Tongue

The long, thin tongue has a sticky tip that is used like a fishing rod to catch and reel in the tree frog's victims.

Eyes

This frog is named for its huge, bulging red eyes. Both eyes have three eyelids. The third eyelid has a special film over it that allows the frog to protect its eyes from danger while still being able to see.

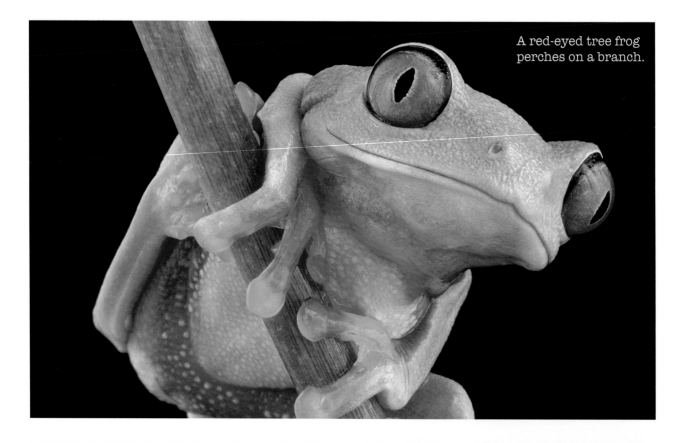

A red-eyed tree frog perches on a branch.

Ferocious Fact

In nature, bright colors can signal to predators that an animal is poisonous. Over time, non-harmful animals have evolved to mimic the appearance of poisonous animals. The red-eyed tree frog is one of these creatures. Its bright colors resemble members of the poison dart frog family, although the red-eyed tree frog isn't poisonous.

The red-eyed tree frog's bright colors often frighten predators that want to eat it.

Even though red-eyed tree frogs are colorful, they are not poisonous.

Did You Know?

- Male red-eyed tree frogs can grow up to 2 in (5 cm) long. Females are a little larger, at up to 3 in (7.5 cm).

- Female tree frogs lay eggs on a leaf above a pond. Once hatched, the newborn tadpoles fall into the water below.

- Tree frog tadpoles feed on fruit flies and pinhead crickets.

Female red-eyed tree frogs lay eggs on leaves.

Glossary

blubber Excessive fat on the bodies of leopard seals, whales, and other animals.

carnivore An animal that eats other animals.

crustaceans Animals, such as lobsters and crabs, that have several pairs of legs and a sectioned body covered in a thick shell.

endangered species Any species threatened with extinction.

krill Small ocean creatures that are a source of food for seals.

larynx Part of the throat that has vocal chords.

predator An animal that hunts other animals.

prehistoric Very old; existing before people could write.

prey An animal picked by another animal to be its food.

retina Sensitive tissue at the back of the eye that detects images and sends signals to the brain about what it can see.

stalk To follow something by moving slowly.

webbed Word used to describe feet, usually of birds such as ducks, whose toes are connected with a layer of skin in between, used for swimming in water.

Find Out More

Do you want to learn more about your favorite animals from this book? Check out these books and websites:

Books

Burnie, David. *Bird.* New York, NY: DK Publishing, 2008.

Ganeri, Anita. *Jaguar. A Day in the Life of Rainforest Animals.* Portsmouth, NH: Heinemann Read and Learn, 2010.

Lopes, Maria L. *Rainforest Animals.* Seattle, WA: Amazon CreateSpace, 2013.

Spelman, Lucy. *National Geographic Animal Encyclopedia.* Washington, DC: National Geographic, 2012.

Websites

Kids' Planet ESPECIES Animal Facts Sheets

www.kidsplanet.org/factsheets/map.html

Learn about different animals by region and unlock information about each animal.

National Geographic's Animal Profiles

kids.nationalgeographic.com/kids/animals

This website is great for looking up more facts about your favorite animals around the world.

Index

carnivore, 26

frigate bird
and flying, 6–9
habitat preferences, 6
physical characteristics, 7
predator habits, 9

jaguar
as a hunter, 14, 16
habitat preferences, 14
physical characteristics, 15
predator habits, 14

leopard seal
as a hunter, 10
habitat preferences, 10
physical characteristics, 11
predator habits, 10, 12–13

leatherback turtle
as a hunter, 18
habitat preferences, 18
laying eggs, 18
physical characteristics, 19

red-eyed tree frog
as a hunter, 26
habitat preferences, 26
physical characteristics, 27
mimics poisonous animals, 28

vine snake
habitat preferences, 22
known species, 25
physical characteristics, 23
predator habits, 22